Prayers of the Faithful

Year B

Hugh McGinlay

Desbooks

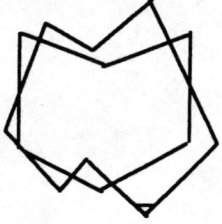

Published by
DESBOOKS
56 Wales Street
Thornbury 3071
Australia

ISBN 0 949824 25 9

Prayers of the Faithful, Year B
© Hugh McGinlay 1996

First printed 1996

Design and setting by Desbooks
Printed by Gill Miller Press, Melbourne

Contents

Introduction

These prayers have been around in various formats for more than three years. First written for use in St Joseph's Parish in Northcote, Victoria, they were later offered to other parishes and schools where priests and other ministers and teachers have found them a useful addition or supplement to more traditional prayers.

The format of the prayers is simple. As a general rule, the four prayers pick up some of the themes of each of the four readings. The first prayer relates to the first reading; the second prayer to the second reading; the third and fourth to the gospel reading for the day. Exceptions happen on major festivals of the church when the theme of the Sunday or festival is reflected in each of the readings.

In writing the prayers, I have been concerned to highlight the Bible teaching in a way that makes it accessible in a prayer form as well as reminding the congregation of the reading they listened to earlier in the service. I have also had in mind that the prayer would use inclusive language as much as possible while remaining faithful to a tradition that has at its heart a belief in God revealed as Father, Son and Spirit.

The lay out of the prayers deliberately uses 'sense lines'. This encourages the reader to read the prayers in ways that makes their meaning easy to understand, suggesting a slight pause at the end of each line.

The prayers are not exhaustive for the Sunday. There is obvilusly room for other petitions - local or universal - and parishes and schools will have their own concerns to mention. They will also know that there is a variety of appropriate response (sung as well as spoken) that can replace the formal 'Lord, hear us' that has been used here.

I gratefully acknowledge the many priests and lay people throughout Australia who have encouraged me in this ministry; I acknowledge in a special way the support of my wife Andrea and my sons Hugh and Danny

Hugh McGinlay
Advent 1996

Advent 1

Priest/leader: 'Be on your guard. Stay awake!'
Advent is a time of waiting -
waiting to celebrate the birth of Jesus.
But also waiting for the coming of the Lord.
In a spirit of openness to what God wants of us,
we recall our needs and the needs of all God's people.

1. For the gift of openness to God
(pause)
God is the potter; we the clay.
In this time of Advent
may we be open to what God wants
taking seriously the command to prepare
for God's coming into our lives.
Lord, hear us.

2. For a gift to understand the meaning of Advent
(pause)
May we continue to grow in faith
in our God who is with us.
May we be alert to the signs of the times,
steady and blameless in our lives
as we wait for the Day of the Lord
Lord, hear us

3. For the gift of patience.
(pause)
May we be good servants
waiting for the return of Jesus our Master.
May we be ready to greet him when he comes
worthy of his confidence in us.
Lord, hear us.

4 For the gift of hope.
(pause)
May we recognise God as Creator
and ruler of our universe.
May we so live according to the gospel
that others may be encouraged to trust in God's power
to bring peace to our world.
Lord, hear us

Priest/leader:
Creator God,
you command us look beyond this present world
to a time when your kingdom will come.
Help us to prepare for your coming
and to look for it with confidence and love.
We ask this through Christ our Lord. Amen.

Advent 1

Advent 2

Priest/leader: 'Prepare a way for the Lord!'
Prepare to let God come into our lives.
Prepare to be changed by what God demands of us.
Moved by the preaching of the Baptist,
we recall our needs before God.

1. For the gift of consolation
(pause)
God promises consolation and peace
to those who follow the way of the Lord.
In this time of Advent,
may we turn to the Lord in prayer and penance
and be filled with the peace that only God can give.
Lord, hear us.

2. We pray for the gift of hope.
(pause)
In a world that is often full of despair,
we ask for the gift of hope,
confident that the God
who led us through exile and bitterness
will be our consolation
and bring us refreshment and new hope.
Lord, hear us.

3. For the gift of repentance
(pause)
May we be aware of our need for repentance
regretting the evil we do to others
and resolving in this time of preparation
that Sin will not control our lives
nor selfishness the values we live by.
Lord, hear us.

4. For a right understanding about what is of value in life.
(pause)
Looking forward to a new heaven and a new earth,
we ask for a right understanding
of what is valuable in God's sight,
not trusting our own understanding
but trusting in God alone.
Lord, hear us.

Priest/leader:
In this time of waiting,
we commend ourselves and our needs
to our God who comforts us
like shepherds comforting their lambs.
Through Christ our Lord. Amen.

Advent 3

Priest/leader: We have listened to God's word
broken for us.
In a spirit of joy, we bring our needs before God.

1. For patience and joy in God's service.
(pause)
May we experience God's gifts of patience and joy
to overcome the hurts we experience
in our world and in our lives.
May we treat other people as God treats us -
with compassion and love-
so that broken hearts may be bound up
and the poor cared for.
Lord, hear us.

2. For the gift of peace.
(pause)
May the God of peace make us perfect and holy
and may we be so renewed in this time of Advent
that we may be eager for the Lord's coming,
prepared by lives of prayer
and holding to what is good.
Lord, hear us.

3. For a willingness to be witnesses to Christ.
(pause)
Like John the Baptist, may we learn to witness
to the light of Christ
not mindful of ourselves
but anxious to point to the One who stands among us
Jesus the Christ, sent by God
to bring us peace and joy.
Lord, hear us.

4 For the gift of being on fire for God.
(pause)
With John the Baptist as our model,
and moved by his enthusiasm for God's promises,
may we be people on fire for God's truth
filled with the Holy Spirit
and eager to live as people of God.
Lord, hear us.

Priest/leader: Creator God,
we rejoice in this time of Advent,
not because the world and all it contains are perfect,
but because we believe in your abiding love,
and look for your Day of Consolation.
Grant what we need through Christ our Lord. Amen.

Advent 3

Advent 4

Priest/leader:
'Do not be afraid!'
As we prepare for the birth of the Messiah at Christmas,
and await the Day of the Lord,
we turn again to our God
whose love we acknowledge
and who is faithful to the promises.

1. For the gift of knowing God's will.
(pause)
Like David, may we be open to God's will for us.
May we not seek to impose our human desires on God
but be aware that God has plans
for the church and the world
that are beyond all human imaginings.
Lord, hear us.

2. For the grace to be ready for Christmas.
(pause)
In these days before Christmas,
may we enter more deeply
into the hidden mysteries of God.
May we so empty ourselves
as to be filled with joy
at the fulfilment of God's promises.
Lord, hear us.

3. For a spirit of wonder.
(pause)
Just as Mary was startled and confused
by the angel's message,
so may we be open to God's surprises
aware that our ways are not God's ways.
Lord, hear us.

4. For joy in celebrating God's good news.
(pause)
May we be filled with joy in this time of Advent
and moved by God's generosity.
May we live lives
that so reflect gospel teachings
that others may come to share our faith and our joy.
Lord, hear us.

Priest/leader: God of the promises,
lift up our hearts,
as we prepare for the birth of the Messiah.
We commend our needs
and the needs of all the world to you.
Through Christ our Lord. Amen.

Advent 4

Christmas

Priest/leader:
'Today a Saviour has been born to us,
Christ the Lord.'
On this holy day,
we have listened with joy to God's good news.
With renewed confidence
we bring before our God
our needs and those of all the world.

1. For joy and peace at Christmas.
(pause)
May this be for us and for all people
a time of joy and peace
and may all the nations of the earth
rejoice at the birth of Christ.
Lord, hear us.

2. For a renewed sense of hope in our world.
(pause)
May our celebration of the birth of Jesus
be an occasion for renewed hope in our world;
and may our joy and our witness
bring the good news of salvation
to the whole human race.
Lord, hear us.

3. For those in sorrow at this time.
(pause)
We recall those who are in sorrow or trouble
at this time -
those who are mourning the loss of family and friends;
those who are homeless and unemployed;
those who are sick.
Lord, hear us.

4. For peace in our families.
(pause)
May we experience peace in our families
at this special time,
and may the spirit of Christmas
be with our families and communities
throughout the year ahead.
Lord, hear us.

Priest/leader: Mighty God and prince of peace,
our hearts are filled with joy and confidence
as we make our prayers to you on this special day,
for you are Lord for ever and ever. Amen.

Christmas

1 January Mary, Mother of God.

Year B

Priest/leader: On this festival of Mary, Mother of God,
we have listened to God's Word
and been nourished by its teaching.
With Mary as our example
we turn to the Lord in prayer.

1. For a true devotion to Mary, Mother of God.
(pause)
Mary is the instrument of God's blessing.
May we learn from her example
by trying to discover what God wants of us
and by lives of gentleness, prayer and service.
Lord, hear us.

2. For the gift of being thankful.
(pause)
May we be aware of the blessings of God in our lives
and with Mary as our mother
thank God for the gift of the Son
to be our Saviour and our brother.
Lord, hear us.

3. For those who care for children in our community.
(pause)
May we always be thankful to God
for those who care for children in our community.
With Mary our mother to guide them
may they be strong in their love
and constant in their care.
Lord, hear us.

4. For an openness towards God.
 (pause)
Mary said yes to God
when the angel asked her to be mother of the Messiah.
May we be open to God's promptings in life
and learn to accept God's purposes
especially in time of trouble.
Lord, hear us.

Priest/leader:
God of all consolation,
we honour Mary, mother of the Saviour and our mother.
Listen to our prayers for we make them
in the name of her Son, Jesus Christ our Lord. Amen

January 1

Epiphany of the Lord

Priest/leader: 'The sight of the star filled them with delight.'
The good news of Jesus' birth
fills us with delight
and we have listened to God's Word broken for us.
Now we approach the Lord of the Universe
for our needs and those of all the world.

1. For peace in our world.
(pause)
May all the nations of the world
receive the light that God sends
and strive for peace in our time -
peace that only God can bring.
Lord, hear us.

2. For a renewed desire to serve in our world.
(pause)
May we who follow the infant King of the Jews
share his life of service
and by our witness to gospel values
bring all people to acknowledge his truth.
Lord, hear us.

3. For the Jewish people.
(pause)
May the people of Israel be faithful
to their ancient covenant with God
and may we who share God's blessing with them
always respect those
who were first to receive God's good news.
Lord, hear us.

4. For a sense of delight in God's presence.
(pause)
May we who celebrate this day
experience joy and delight in the presence of our king
and by the honesty and integrity of our lives
be faithful disciples of the Lord we worship.
Lord, hear us.

Priest/leader:
God of the universe.
your good news is for all the peoples of the earth.
Hear our prayers this day and grant what we need.
Through Christ our Lord. Amen.

Epiphany

Ash Wednesday

Priest/leader: 'Turn from your sins
and believe the good news!'
This is God's Word to us today.
We have listened to that Word
and we turn to God in prayer.

1. For the grace to follow Christ
   in this journey through Lent.
(pause)
As we begin our forty days of Lent,
we ask God to raise in our minds
an awareness of sin in our lives
and the greatness of God's tender love.
Lord, hear us,

2. For the grace to take the journey seriously.
(pause)
We beg God's blessing on our journey
to help us take stock of our lives:
 - what is important for us
 - what controls us
 - what we need to do
to be faithful to the gospel and followers of Christ.
Lord, hear us.

3. For the grace to grow in prayer.
(pause)
We ask the Lord to give us a spirit of prayer
that we might relish the time we spend in prayer,
not regarding it as a burden
but a time of joy and reflection
in the presence of the God who loves us.
Lord, hear us.

4. For a true spirit of penance during Lent.
(pause)
May we learn to follow the teaching of Jesus
disciplining ourselves by prayer, fasting and acts of charity
so that we might have a true understanding
of what is of lasting value in life
according to the mind of our Saviour.
Lord, hear us.

Priest/leader: Creator God,
our bodies have been marked with the ashes of repentance.
May these be a reminder to us to be strong and constant
in our journey through Lent.
Listen to the prayers, help us in what we need.
Through Christ our Lord. Amen.

Lent 1

Priest/leader :
"The time has come! God's rule is at hand!'
Strengthened by God's Word
we turn to God our Creator
for strength and perseverance
in our observance of Lent.

1. For a renewed understanding
of God's covenant with the world.
(pause)
Recalling God's covenant with Noah
and the promise made to the world,
may we grow in our understanding
of God's love for the world and all its people.
Lord, hear us.

2. For an awareness of the power of sin in our lives.
(pause)
Jesus was tempted
to abandon the life God had chosen for him.
May we resist sin in our lives,
and by the values we choose,
remain faithful to the way of Christ.
Lord, hear us.

3. For a desire to walk in God's way.
(pause)
We ask God's help in choosing to walk
the paths of truth and integrity and justice.
Even when we stray from those ideals,
may we be comforted by God's constant love.
Lord, hear us.

4. For an eagerness to proclaim God's good news.
(pause)
May we be alert to the signs of the times
looking for ways to proclaim
God's good news to all the world
by lives that are faithful to God's teaching
and values that reflect God's Word.
Lord, hear us.

Priest/leader :
God of all comfort
you sent your angels to comfort Jesus your son
and strengthen his desire to do your will.
Strengthen us, we pray,
so that we may be faithful followers
of your teaching.
We ask this through Christ Our Lord. Amen.

Lent 1

Lent 2

Priest/leader :
'With God on our side,
who can be against us?'
Strengthened by God's Word
we turn to the Lord,
aware of our needs in the church
and in the world.

1. For a deeper awareness of God's faithfulness and love.
(pause)
In a world that is often in shadow
and filled with the power of darkness,
may we always be confident
of God's faithfulness and love
and be people of hope and trust.
Lord, hear us.

2. For a desire to do God's will always.
(pause)
May we learn to be people of deep faith in God
eager to do what God wants of us in life.
With Abraham as our father in faith
may we too be faithful to the covenant.
Lord, hear us.

3. For a renewal in our commitment to the way of Christ.
(pause)
Following God's command, may we learn to listen to the
Beloved Son
so that by obeying his teaching
we may, like him, lead lives transformed by God.
Lord, hear us.

4. For a sense of wonder in the presence of God.
(pause)
Like Peter and James and John,
may we be so filled with delight
in the presence of God
that we welcome God's presence in our lives.
Lord, hear us.

Priest/leader :
God of the transfiguration,
fill us with your love and comfort.
Make us eager to listen to your Son
and to follow his way,
even to death and resurrection,
We ask this through Christ our Lord .Amen

Lent 3

Priest/leader :
'The law of the Lord is perfect
and God's way is worthy of our trust.'
We have shared God's Word
and reflected on its message.
We now ask our God
for what we need to be faithful to that teaching.

1.For a deeper understanding of God's law.
(pause)
May we receive the gift of wisdom
 to understand God's law and God's way
not simply as revealed to a people long ago
but given to us to live out
in our time.
Lord, hear us.

2. For a sense of discipline in our lives.
(pause)
May we learn from Christ crucified
to be more aware of other people;
and by fasting and self disipline
may we be moved by the needs of others
in our country and in our world.
Lord, hear us.

3. For an awareness of our need for God.
(pause)
May we learn to find time for God in our lives:
making time for prayer and reflection;
especially in times of trouble and despair.
Lord, hear us.

4. For a renewal of zeal among God's people.
(pause)
May we be constant in living as God's people
in the church and in the community.
May we be faithful in our concerns
for God's teaching and God's truth
and be zealous witnesses
to the way of Christ.
Lord, hear us.

Priest/leader :
God of all compassion,
we renew our trust in you.
Fill us with zeal for your teaching
that people everywhere may come to know you
and live as you would have them live.
We ask this through Christ our Lord .Amen

Lent 3

Lent 4

Priest/leader :
'The Son lifted up on the cross
is the measure of God's love for the world.'
On our journey through Lent,
we recall God's generous love
and bring before the Lord
our fears, our hopes,
our concerns and our needs.

1. For a deeper faith in God's activity in our world.
(pause)
God inspired Cyrus, King of Persia
to console the Jewish people
in their time of exile;
may we renew our faith
in God's saving presence in our world.
Lord, hear us.

2. For a greater awareness of God's generous love.
(pause)
We hope in God because God is faithful
and we trust in God's generous love.
May we show forth God's goodness
in how we live and what we value.
Lord, hear us.

3. For a spirit of self-giving.
(pause)
Jesus gave himself for all of us
when he was lifted up on the cross.
May we share his spirit of self-giving
and be generous with what we have,
overcoming the darkness of greed
by the light of our concern.
Lord, hear us.

4.For an eagerness to walk in the light.
(pause)
May we be people who walk in the light of Christ,
avoiding the darkness
and being filled with the light that comes from God.
Lord, hear us.

Priest/leader :
God of light,
you command us to prefer light to darkness.
Help us to overcome sin in our lives
and so live by the truth of the gospel.
We ask this through Christ our Lord .Amen

Year B

Lent 5

Priest/leader:
When I am lifted up from the earth
I will draw all people to myself.
Our eyes are on the Christ of God -
Jesus, soon to be crucified.
Aware of our sinfulness but full of confidence
we bring before God our needs
and those of the whole people of God.

1. For an increased desire to obey God.
(pause)
You have taught us that Jesus learned obedience
through suffering.
By our obedience and our desire to do God's will
may we experience the peace that God alone can give.
Lord, hear us

2. For a deeper understanding of God's covenant of love.
(pause)
God has written the covenant on our hearts.
May our understanding of that covenant
make us eager to live God's commandments
with honesty, integrity and faithfulness.
Lord, hear us.

3. For a rich harvest among God's people.
(pause)
We believe that the death
of a single grain of wheat can yield a rich harvest.
May we so die to self and live for others
that the world may turn from selfishness,
and enjoy a harvest of peace, security and justice.
Lord, hear us.

4. For a spirit of service.
(pause)
May we be good servants of the Lord,
looking for ways to be of service
in the community and in the church,
responding to those in need as the Lord showed
in his life and in his death.
Lord, hear us.

Priest/leader:
God of love and service
your Son died to bring a rich harvest of life for others.
Awaken in us a desire to be servants like him
and to be always faithful
to the covenant you have written in our hearts.
We ask this through Christ our Lord. Amen.

Lent 5

Lent 6 (Passion/Palm Sunday)

Priest/leader:
We have begun our Holy Week observances.
We have celebrated Jesus' entry to Jerusalem
and watched the mood change from joy to sadness.
Yet in a spirit of hope, we present our needs before our
God.

1. For Christian people everywhere.
(pause)
At the beginning of this Holy Week,
we pray for all our Christian brothers and sisters
that we may follow the example of Jesus
who emptied himself for us.
May we learn to be one with each other
in the service of all.
Lord, hear us.

2. For those who suffer for what they believe.
(pause)
We pray for those in our world
who, like Jesus, are unjustly persecuted
for what they hold dearest.
By our prayers and actions,
may we be in solidarity with them
who suffer for justice and truth.
Lord, hear us.

3. For a sense of peace in the midst of suffering.
(pause)
May we be granted the gift of inner peace
when we experience pain at the hands of others.
And may Christians everywhere
support those who are suffering
by our prayers and understanding and love.
Lord, hear us.

4. For a fruitful observance of Holy Week
(pause)
May we use this Holy Week profitably
- for reflection and prayer
- for renewal and repentance
- for acts of charity
- for worship and sharing.
Lord, hear us.

Priest/leader:
God of compassion,
keep us faithful even in times of suffering
and bring us to Easter joy.
We ask this through Christ our Lord. Amen.

Year B

Holy Thursday

Year B

Priest/leader: On this holy night
we remember with joy the Supper of the Lord.
Gathered as God's people
and refreshed by the breaking of God's Word
we recall our needs
and the needs of the church.

1. For a spirit of service.
(pause)
Jesus the Master washed the feet
of his disciples.
May we learn from him that God's ways
demands service of others
in the community and in the church.
Lord, hear us.

2. For those called to ministry in the churches.
(pause)
May all who are ordained to ministry in the churches
be wise leaders in the community,
people of integrity and faith
eager to share God's Word
with their fellow servants in the church.
Lord, hear us.

3. For a renewal in our following of Christ.
(pause)
Jesus gave us a new commandment
to love one another has he loved us.
May we deepen our desire to live that commandment
that people everywhere may recognise us
as followers of Christ.
Lord, hear us.

4. For a desire to be broken for others.
(pause)
May the broken bread and the outpoured wine
be symbols of God's people
willing to be broken and poured out
for the service of the world.
Lord, hear us.

Priest/leader:
Ruler of the Universe, God most high,
we thank you for your love
for all the world.
Give us the strength we need
to be your faithful witnesses.
We ask this through Christ our Lord. Amen.

Holy Thursday

Year B

General Intercessions for Good Friday

1. For the church
Let us pray for God's church all over the world.
(pause)
Lord, guide your church throughout the world.
May the church proclaim your good news
and bring your salvation to all people.
We ask this through Christ our Lord. Amen.

2. For the leaders in the churches,
Let us pray for the leaders in the Christian churches:
for the Pope, the patriarchs of the Orthodox Churches,
the Archbishop of Canterbury, and
the leaders of the Protestant Churches.
(pause)
Lord, guide the Pope
and all the leaders in the churches.
May their preaching and their example
help us grow in faith
and become more faithful followers of your son.
We ask this through Christ our Lord. Amen.

3. For all members of the churches.
Let us pray for all who belong
to the people of God.
(pause)
Lord, your Spirit guides the church
and makes it holy.
Help us to be faithful witnesses
to the way of Jesus
in what we do and what we value.
We ask this through Christ our Lord. Amen.

4. For those preparing for Baptism.
Let us pray for those people
who are preparing for Baptism.
(pause)
Lord, you constantly bless your church
with new members.
Increase the faith and understanding of those
preparing for Baptism at this time.
We ask this through Christ our Lord. Amen.

5. For unity among Christians.
Let us pray for Christian unity
(pause)
Look with favour on all
who follow the way of your Son
and share the same Baptism
Bring us all to the fullness of faith
and keep us one in the bonds of love.
We ask this through Christ our Lord. Amen.

Good
Friday

6. For the Jewish people.
Let us pray for the Jewish people
the first to hear God's Word
and share the covenant.
(pause)
Lord, long ago you gave the promises
to Abraham and to his descendants for ever.
We pray for our Jewish brothers and sisters
as they strive to be faithful to your covenant with them.
We ask this through Christ our Lord. Amen.

7. For those who not believe in Christ.
Let us pray for those
who do not believe in Christ
that they may be shown the way to salvation.
(pause)
We pray for our brothers and sisters
who do not acknowledge Christ in their hearts.
By our witness to his teaching, may they discover
the truth about Jesus and walk in his ways.
We ask this through Christ our Lord. Amen.

8. For those who do not believe in God.
Let us pray for those who do not believe in God
that they may find God by following
what is right in their hearts.
(pause)
Lord, you created people to know you
and enjoy peace in your love.
May our faithfulness in reflecting your love and mercy
bring those who do not believe in you
to acknowledge you as Lord and God of all.
We ask this through Christ our Lord. Amen.

9. For those in public office.
Let us pray for those who serve the community
in public office.
(pause)
Lord, in your goodness, watch over those in public office
so that people everywhere
may know freedom, security and peace.
We ask this through Christ our Lord. Amen.

10. For those in special need.
Let us pray for the sick, the dying,
those who suffer in war and famine
and all who need our prayers at this time.
(pause)
Lord, give strength to the weary
and new courage to those who have lost heart.
We commend to you all who are in need.
We ask this through Christ our Lord. Amen.

Easter Vigil

Priest/leader:
The Lord is risen! heaven and earth rejoice
in the reconciliation of God
with all creation.
Filled with Easter joy
we bring to God our needs
for the church and for the world.

1. For the community that is called the church.
(pause)
We are an Easter people
and we ask God's blessing on the church.
May it be a source of joy and hope
in a world that is often full of despair.
Lord, hear us.

2. For new Christians
(pause)
May those who have been baptised this night
know the peace that only God can give
and may they be faithful to the promises
they have made.
Lord, hear us.

3. For a deeper faith in the risen Christ.
(pause)
By the death if Jesus, sin has been destroyed
and has power over us no longer.
Strengthened by faith
may we live no longer as slaves of sin
but alive for God in Christ Jesus.
Lord, hear us.

4. For the world in darkness.
(pause)
May the light of Christ so shine
in our lives and in the church
that people everywhere will be comforted
by our charity and our kindness.
Lord, hear us.

Priest/leader:
Creator God of heaven and earth,
we bless you and thank you for this holy night.
Be with us always and help us be faithful witnesses
to the risen Christ.
We ask this through Christ our Lord. Amen.

Easter Vigil

Easter Day

Christ our hope is risen! Alleluia!
In our rejoicing at the resurrection of our Saviour,
we turn to God and recall our needs
and those of all the church.

1. For the church throughout the world.
(pause)
May Christians everywhere
experience the joy of the risen Christ
and be renewed in faith and hope.
Lord, hear us.

2. For those in trouble at this time.
(pause)
May the triumph of Christ over death
be a comfort to those who are in distress
or are suffering at this time.
Lord, hear us.

3, For a desire to live a new life in Christ.
(pause)
May this Easter Day
inspire us to grow in Christ
so that like him
we may choose to walk in the light
and avoid the darkness of sin.
Lord, hear us.

4. For a commitment to be witnesses to Christ.
(pause)
May we share the enthusiasm of Mary Magdalene
to be witnesses to the resurrection of Jesus
by our faithfulness to his teaching
and our living of gospel values.
Lord, hear us.

Priest/leader: God of all hope,
you raised Jesus to newness of life.
Send your Spirit into our hearts
that even in troubled times,
we may be people of hope.
Through Christ our Lord. Amen.

Easter Day

Easter 2

Priest/leader:
'Happy are those who have not seen yet believe!'
In our Easter celebrations
we have listened to the Word
and professed our faith.
Now we remember the needs of the church
and the world
as we turn to God in prayer.

1.For a deeper commitment
   to the community called church.
(pause)
The earliest Christians practised charity
and care for one another.
May we too deepen our understanding of community
so that we may be moved to action
for those in our world who are in need.
Lord, hear us.

2. For the needs of others in our country
    and our community.
(pause)
May we live out Easter joy in our country
and local community,
alert to the needs and sufferings of others
and concerned for those who are sick
or bereaved, homeless or neglected.
Lord, hear us.

3. For the gift of being peacemakers
(pause)
Peace is the gift of the risen Christ
to his church and his people.
May we be bearers of that precious gift
in our families and communities.
Lord, hear us.

4. For a readiness to forgive.
(pause)
The risen Jesus commanded us to forgive one another.
Like him, may we forgive those who condemn us
and look for ways to be reconciled
with those whom we have offended.
Lord, hear us.

Priest/leader:
Having died with Christ may we now live with him,
eager to obey the commands of God
and to forgive one another.
We ask this through Christ our Lord Amen.

Easter 2

Easter 3

Priest/leader:
'We cannot know God
unless we keep God's commandments.'
We have listened to the Word broken for us
and now with confidence we approach our God
for the needs of our community.

1. For a deeper awareness of Christ present among us.
(pause)
The disciples recognised Christ
in the breaking of the bread.
May we who gather in his name
learn to recognise his presence among us,
giving us strength to live as he commanded.
Lord, hear us.

2. For the gift of peace.
(pause)
Aware of Christ's presence among us today
may we receive the gift of peace
in the church and in the world,
in our families and communities.
Lord, hear us.

3. For an understanding of God's Word.
(pause)
May we grow in the love and understanding
of God's Word.
May it be for us a continuing source of prayer
and consolation and strength.
Lord, hear us.

4. For the joy of being witnesses to Christ.
(pause)
May we be faithful followers of Christ
in our daily lives;
and by our love for one another
and the gospel values we proclaim,
may God's name be glorified
and people come to know the good news
about God's love for all the world.
Lord, hear us.

Priest/leader:
May we be strong in faith and hope and love,
recognising Christ's presence among us
and renewed in our desire
to live as God wants.
We ask this through Christ our Lord Amen.

Easter 3

Easter 4

Priest/leader:
'I am the good shepherd.'
Strengthened by God's Word
and God's promises,
we recall our needs
and the needs of the church..

1. For the leaders in the churches.
(pause)
With Jesus the good shepherd as their model,
may the leaders in the churches
be faithful preachers and teachers of God's way.
Lord, hear us.

2. For a greater understanding of God's choices.
(pause)
The stone that the builders rejected
has become the corner stone.
May we grow to appreciate
the mystery of God's choices
relying on gospel teaching
and the example of the good shepherd.
Lord, hear us.

3. For a response in our lives to God's love.
(pause)
God's love for us is so lavish
that we have become God's children.
May this knowledge fill us with confidence
and help us to overcome fear and despair in life.
Lord, hear us.

4. For those who need our help in the community.
(pause)
In Jesus' name,
Peter brought the gift of healing.
May we too reach out to others in need
and by our faith in Christ and his power to save
bring healing and wholeness to those in the community.
Lord, hear us.

Priest/leader:
God, may we be faithful in our following
of Christ the good shepherd
so that others may be moved
to belong to the flock of Christ.
We ask this through Christ our Lord Amen.

Easter 4

Easter 5

Priest/leader:
'Jesus is the true vine and we are the branches.'
Strengthened by God's Word,
we call to mind our needs
for ourselves and our community.

1. For an awareness of the closeness of Christ.
(pause)
In this Easter time, we have become a new people.
May we learn to cherish
our closeness to Christ
so that his life may influence
all that we say and do.
Lord, hear us.

2. For boldness in being witnesses to Christ.
(pause)
Paul proclaimed his faith in Christ
boldly and without fear.
May we too be faithful witnesses
of the risen Christ
by the honesty of our actions,
and our faithfulness to gospel values.
Lord, hear us.

3. For a desire to keep God's commandments.
(pause)
Our love for God is shown
by what we do and how we live.
May those who belong to the community
that is called the church
be marked by a desire to be faithful
to God's commandments.
Lord, hear us.

4. For the will to bear fruit for God.
(pause)
May we grow in our desire
to live the Christian way,
imitating Christ in his life and teaching
and sharing his concern for the poor and the outcast.
Lord, hear us.

Priest/leader:
God of all faithfulness,
you bless your people always.
Grant that we may be eager to do your will in all things
and bear fruit to your glory.
We ask this through Christ our Lord Amen.

Easter 5

Easter 6

Priest/leader:
'You are my friends if you do what I command you.'
As friends of Jesus,
we have listened to God's Word, broken for us.
Now we turn to our God in prayer
confident that we will be heard.

1. For an awareness of God's love for all people.
(pause)
God has no favourites
and no nation or people can claim God as their own.
May we learn tolerance,
acknowledging that all
who seek justice and truth in their lives
are acceptable to God.
Lord, hear us.

2. For the gift of loving one another.
(pause)
May we take to heart the command to love
learning from the example of Jesus himself.
May we try to live out this command
in lives of sincerity and integrity
seeking justice and truth and peace.
Lord, hear us.

3. For a deeper understanding of God's love for us.
(pause)
God's love is measured by the gift of Jesus, God's son.
May we grow in understanding
the meaning of this great love
and respond to it by our own self-giving.
Lord, hear us.

4. For a desire to deepen our friendship with God.
(pause)
We are no longer servants but friends of the Lord.
May our friendship with God deepen
and grow to that perfection that God wants of us.
Lord, hear us.

Priest/leader:
God of love,
you command us to love on another.
Help us increase in our faith life,
and grow in our love for one another.
We ask this through Christ our Lord Amen.

Easter 6

Ascension Day

Priest/leader:
'God has put all things under his feet
and made him ruler of everything.'
As followers of Christ
rejoicing in his glorious ascension,
we come to God in prayer,
remembering our needs
and those of God's people everywhere.

1. For a deepening sense of hope
(pause)
In all that happens in our lives and in our world,
may we be consoled
by the knowledge of God's faithfulness,
and assured of sharing
the glory that is Christ's.
Lord, hear us.

2. For a greater awareness of God's plan of salvation.
(pause)
May we who are members of Christ's body, the church,
grow in understanding the mystery
of God's purpose for the world
and may we so live as God's people
that we may share the glory that has been promised.
Lord, hear us.

3. For a desire to be witnesses to the gospel
(pause)
May we be faithful witnesses to Christ
and to all that the gospel teaches
so that people everywhere
may understand God's love for all the world.
Lord, hear us.

4. For an appreciation of the signs God gives us in life.
(pause)
The Word of God is accompanied by signs and wonders.
May we become more aware of the wonderful things
God does in the lives of people
helping us respond to the preaching of the Word
by gospel values of love and forgiveness
and a thirst for justice for all.
Lord, hear us.

Priest/leader:
God of the promises, we worship you
as our ruler and head.
Be our consolation as we await the coming of the Lord.
We ask this through Christ our Lord Amen.

Year B

Easter 7

Priest/leader:
We are the Easter people.
Strengthened and renewed by the Word of God,
broken for us,
we bring before our God
our needs and the needs of all the church.

1. For a profound faith in God's love for us.
(pause)
The measure of God's love is that
the Son was sent to die for us.
May we realise the great love God has for each of us
and be comforted always by our faith.
Lord, hear us.

2. For a desire to love one another as God commands.
(pause)
God lives in those who love
and the command is to love one another.
May we take to heart this command,
showing forth our love
by actions of charity
and forgiveness and understanding.
Lord, hear us.

3. For those called to be teachers and preachers in the church.
(pause)
Like Matthias, may teachers and preachers
be people of integrity and faith,
eager to witness to the good news about Jesus
and supported by the prayers
and encouragement of all the churches.
Lord, hear us.

4. For a commitment to live by the truth.
(pause)
May we be constant in using gospel teaching
and the example of Jesus
to resist false values
and unjust systems in our world.
Lord, hear us.

Priest/leader:
God of love,
consecrate your people in truth;
Keep us true to your name.
Help us to love as you command
so that we may share your joy to the full.
We ask this through Christ our Lord Amen.

Easter 7

Pentecost Day

Priest/leader:
Fifty days have passed since Easter.
We welcome God's Spirit among us
comforting, inspiring, consoling
and helping us as we pray to God
for what we need.

1. For an openness to God's Holy Spirit.
(pause)
The Spirit brings new life to the church
and renews the whole world.
May we be open to the promptings of the Spirit
and accept that the church is led by God's Spirit
towards the future known only to God.
Lord, hear us.

2. For a desire to make Christ known throughout the world.
(pause)
The people of Jerusalem heard the good news
in their own languages.
May we be constant in searching for ways
to make God known by language and preaching
that makes sense to people of today.
Lord, hear us.

3. For a spirit of forgiveness.
(pause)
The gift of the Holy Spirit is a gift of reconciliation.
May we reach out to our brothers and sisters
with forgiveness and tolerance
and be peace makers in our families,
our communities and our world.
Lord, hear us.

4. For a sense of renewal.
(pause)
The Spirit is God's gift for the renewal of the world.
May we grow in prayer; increase in faith;
and be ready to work
for what is good and just and holy
in the church and in our world.
Lord, hear us.

Priest/leader:
Come, Holy Spirit,
fill us with your loving presence.
Make us strong and constant followers of Christ,
on fire, like the apostles,
with desire to proclaim the gospel and to live it out.
We ask this through Christ our Lord. Amen.

Trinity Sunday

Priest/leader:
Everyone who is moved by God's Spirit
is not God's slave but God's child.
As children of God we approach our God
with confidence and without fear,
asking for those things we need
as God's people in God's world.

1. For a respect for the name of God
(pause)
We worship God - three yet one -
and we praise the name of God.
May our love for God
and our concern for God's creation
shine out in our world.
Lord, hear us.

2. For trust in the faithfulness of God
(pause)
May we live in reverence of the Lord,
our help and our shield
and place all our hope in God.
Lord, hear us

3. For a childlike spirit in our attitude to God.
(pause)
We are God's children, chosen in Christ our brother.
May we reverence our God with wonder
but be filled with confidence and trust.
Lord, hear us.

4. For a sense of God's presence.
(pause)
As we live in response to God's commands
may we be more and more aware
that the Lord will be with us to the end of time.
Lord, hear us.

Priest/leader:
Creator God, may your name be held holy!
May your kingdom come!
Listen to the prayers we make this day
through Christ our Lord. Amen.

Body and Blood of Christ

Priest/leader:
Jesus is our high priest,
whose precious blood
has established for us
an everlasting covenant with God.
As people of the covenant,
we bring our prayers before the Lord.

1. For a deeper awareness of God's covenant of love.
(pause)
The people of Israel sealed the covenant with God
using the blood of chosen animals.
May we learn from the shedding of Christ's blood
how great is the love of God
for all the people of the world.
Lord, hear us.

2. For a greater understanding of the sacrifice of Christ.
(pause)
The blood of Christ makes us holy before God.
May we grow in our understanding
of what Christ achieved for us
by his life and death.
May our sharing in the sacrament
increase our service to God and one another.
Lord, hear us.

3. For a love of the Eucharist.
(pause)
Jesus commanded us to share his body and blood
in memory of him.
May we learn to love this central act of worship
and to live out its command of love
in all that we do.
Lord, hear us.

4. For a desire to be more faithful to the covenant.
(pause)
We are nourished by the body and blood of the Lord.
May our sharing in this sacrament
make us active in living out
the Lord's command to love one another.
Lord, hear us.

Priest/leader:
God of the covenant,
you give us this sacrament as a sign of your love for us.
May we grow in love, eager to worship you
by our care for one another.
We ask this through Christ our Lord Amen.

Body and
Blood of Christ

Year B

Sunday 2

Priest/leader :
'Speak, Lord, your servant is listening.'
God's word has been spoken to us
and, like Samuel, we must listen to its message.
We now turn to the God of our ancestors
for what we need in church and community

For a desire to listen to God's Word.
(pause)
May we be open to God's teaching
in the Bible, in the church and in the community
so that we may respond with eagerness
to what is commanded of God's people.
Lord, hear us.

2. For a right attitude to our bodies.
(pause)
May we acknowledge our bodies as a gift of God,
not abusing them or despising them
but treating them with respect and moderation
as temples of God's Holy Spirit.
Lord, hear us.

3. For a desire to follow Christ.
(pause)
Jesus called the apostles to follow him.
May we be faithful followers of our Lord
attentive to his teaching
and living according to the gospel.
Lord, hear us.

4. For a desire to teach others the way of Christ
(pause)
May we be teachers of others
in the way of faith,
passing on what is important in life
by what we value and how we live.
Lord, hear us.

Priest/leader:
God of the promises,
you sent Jesus, the lamb of God,
to be our teacher and guide.
Help us to be faithful to your teaching.
Through Christ our Lord. Amen.

Sunday 2

Sunday 3

Priest/leader: 'Repent and believe the good news.'
This is the first teaching of the Christ.
Nourished by his Word broken for us
we turn to our God
seeking what we need in the church and in the community.

1. For a desire to repond to the gospel
(pause)
The people of Nineveh responded
to the preaching of Jonah,
choosing to follow the way of the Lord.
May we too be conscious of the power of sin in our lives
and refuse to be controlled by it
Lord, hear us.

2. For an appreciation of what is of value in life
(pause)
Paul teaches us about the shortness of life,
and the need to make serious choices.
May we learn to appreciate what is of lasting value in life
and lead lives that are acceptable to our God.
Lord, hear us.

3. For an awareness of the power of God in our world
(pause)
The command to turn from sin
is made to all of us.
May we acknowledge the attraction of evil and selfishness
and resolve, by God's grace,
to resist it in our lives.
Lord, hear us.

4. For a desire to follow the Christ.
(pause)
Like the first disciples
may we be eager to follow the Christ
and by our lifestyle and values
teach others about the kingdom of God.
Lord, hear us.

Priest/leader :
God of all consolation,
you command us to follow your Son.
Help us to be good disciples
in what we do and what we teach.
We ask this through Christ our Lord. Amen.

Sunday 3

Year B

Sunday 4

Priest/leader :
Jesus taught with authority -
and we have listened to his teaching.
Strengthened in faith by its message,
we ask our God for what we need.

1. For prophets in our world.
(pause)
May we be alert to the prophets in our world -
in the church and in the community -
and may we be moved by their teaching
to pay heed to what God wants
in the church and in the world.
Lord, hear us.

2. For a sense of balance in life.
(pause)
Paul commands us to be careful in what we do
finding time for God in the busyness of life.
May we be attentive to the needs of others
eager to show our love for God
in our concern for those we care for.
Lord, hear us.

3. For a desire to be led by the Gospel.
(pause)
May we listen to the teaching of the Gospel
recognising it as the authentic word of our God
and may our lives and what we hope for
reflect its message in all that we do.
Lord, hear us.

4. For an appreciation of Jesus the teacher.
(pause)
May we look to the Lord Jesus
who taught the people with authority
and may his teaching console us
in times of anxiety and trouble.
Lord, hear us.

Priest/leader:
God, the source of all good things,
we thank you for Christ the good teacher.
Help us be faithful to his message
and grant what we need.
Through Christ our Lord. Amen.

Sunday 4

Sunday 5

Priest/leader :
'I came to preach the good news.'
God's Word has been broken for us
and we are strengthened by its message.
We ask our God to look kindly on us
and to grant what we need.

1. For the grace to avoid despair in life.
(pause)
May we not, like Job,
give in to despair in life,
overcome by the pointlessness of it all.
Rather may we acknowledge that God is the ruler of our world
and has a purpose for all of us in life.
Lord, hear us.

2. For a desire to spread the Gospel.
(pause)
Like Paul, may we be enthusiastic about the Gospel -
living by its teaching, and witnessing to its values -
so that people everywhere will be attracted to the Christ
and find freedom and purpose in all that they do
Lord, hear us.

3. For a desire to be of service.
(pause)
May we take Jesus as our model in life,
and by our concern for others,
witness to his teaching in the church
and in the community.
Lord, hear us.

4. For a sense of balance in life.
(pause)
May we look for time to be alone with our God
seeking God's will through prayer and silence
so that our daily lives will not be empty
but filled with a desire to live as God commands.
Lord, hear us.

Priest/leader :
God of the promise,
you fill us with joy in your presence.
Grant what we need in the church
and in the community
for we ask in the name of Jesus the Lord. Amen.

Sunday 6

Priest/leader :
'Be cured!'
Jesus' word of healing to the leper
brings consolation to all of us.
Strengthened by that Word
we ask our God for what we need.

1. For those on the margins of society.
(pause)
We pray for those whom society rejects
- especially in our country and community.
May we be people of compassion
reaching out to welcome those
whom society calls worthless.
Lord, hear us.

2. For a desire to imitate Christ.
(pause)
May we be followers of Christ
in deed and in thought
careful to avoid hurting others
by attitudes that are offensive
and language that discriminates.
Lord, hear us.

3. For a desire to be healers in society.
(pause)
Jesus is our model
of healing, of acceptance, of tolerance.
Like him, may we be healers in society
accepting people who are different from ourselves
in language, culture, and faith.
Lord, hear us.

4. For a desire to spread the good news
(pause)
All of us experience the healing love of God
expressed to us in the care of others.
By what we profess and how we live,
may we declare to others our faith in the Good News
of God's Love and acceptance for all peoples.
Lord, hear us.

Priest/leader :
God of all peoples
You are the Saviour of all the world.
Listen to our prayers and grant what we need.
Through Christ our Lord. Amen.

Sunday 6

Sunday 7

Priest/leader :
'We have never seen anything like this.'
We share the response of those who were witnesses
and we share their joy at the good news
we have received.
Now we ask our God for what we need.

1. For joy that our sins are forgiven.
(pause)
God declares our sins are forgiven,
refusing to recall our deeds in the past.
May our joy in experiencing God's forgiveness
encourage us to avoid sin in our lives
and to live by the Gospel.
Lord, hear us.

2. For joy in following the Lord.
(pause)
We rejoice that God's 'yes' to Christ
includes us who have been baptised in him.
May we be accepting of others,
unselfish in our attitude to them
as God is unselfish toward us.
Lord, hear us.

3.For joy in the power of forgiveness.
(pause)
As we have been forgiven by God
may we be forgiving towards others;
not bearing grudges for past mistakes
- especially in our families -
and willing, like our God, to forget evil that is past.
Lord, hear us.

4. For joy in God's power to save.
(pause)
May we be people of joy,
blessed by the God who saves us.
And may we be faithful followers of the Christ
whose teaching shows us how to live.
Lord, hear us.

Priest/leader :
God of mercy,
have pity on all your children.
Keep us faithful to the way of Christ
and grant what we need.
Through Christ our Lord. Amen.

Year B

Sunday 8

Priest/leader :
'New wine needs fresh skins.'
God's Word is always new -
refreshing us with its message
and calling us to new responses in life.
We turn to our God for help
for what we need.

1. For integrity in our lives.
(pause)
God's love for the people
is intense and everlasting.
May our response to that love
be reflected in lives of integrity and justice,
with a special care for the poor in our world.
Lord, hear us.

2. For a desire to witness to the Gospel.
(pause)
God's love for us
is renewed in every generation.
May we be faithful followers of the Christ,
confident that God's Spirit
gives us the strength to witness to the Gospel.
Lord, hear us.

3. For an openness to what God wants
(pause)
May we be confident in God's love
for the church and the world,
not afraid of the future
or the changes that God has planned for us.
Lord, hear us.

4. For tolerance of the opinions of others.
(pause)
May we be tolerant of each other
in the church and in society
acknowledging that only God is all truth
and that the search for God's way
is sometimes difficult to discern.
Lord, hear us.

Priest/leader :
God of thepromises,
you console us with your love.
Grant what we need
in the church and in society.
Through Christ our Lord. Amen

Sunday 8

Sunday 9

Priest/leader :
'The Son of Man is Master of the Sabbath'
God's Word has been broken for us
and its Good News comforts us in life.
Strengthened by its teaching
We turn to our God
for what we need.

1. For a sense of balance in our lives.
(pause)
God commands us to keep Sabbath,
May we learn to keep a balance in our lives
acknowledging our littleness in God's sight
and the need for rest and quiet
from work and noise.
Lord, hear us.

2. For the sense of God's protection.
(pause)
Paul teaches that God's power is at work in us.
May his teaching comfort and strengthen us
especially when we are troubled in our lives.
Lord, hear us.

3. For a right attitude to the Lord's Day
(pause)
May we acknowledge God's presence
and purpose in our world,
taking time for prayer and worship and recreation;
and by our observance of the Lord's Day
may we witness to what is of lasting importance in life.
Lord, hear us.

4. For a desire to be of service to others
(pause)
The Sabbath is the Lord's and ours too.
May our worship of God and the faith we profess
be reflected in lives that care for others
in the church and in the community.
Lord, hear us.

Priest/leader :
Lord God of the Sabbath
We bless you and thank you for your gift of rest
Grant what we need to be good servants of your son
For he is Lord, for ever and ever. Amen

Sunday 9

Year B

Sunday 10

Priest/leader:
'Those who do God's will
are my mother and brothers and sisters.'
Strengthened by God's Word,
we are confident in bringing before the Lord
our needs and those of all God's people.

1. For confidence that God's promises will be fulfilled.
(pause)
Even from the beginning, after the fall,
God promised that evil would be crushed.
We ask for confidence in God's power
to fulfil all that has been promised.
Lord, hear us.

2. For a sense of hope for the future.
(pause)
The future is known to God alone,
and those who are faithful
are promised a home that lasts forever.
May we be confident of God's love
now and in the future.
Lord, hear us.

3. For unity among God's people.
(pause)
A divided household cannot be strong.
We pray for unity in the community
that is God's church;
and for the gift of love
to temper our judgments about others.
Lord, hear us.

4. For a desire to do God's will.
(pause)
Those who belong to God's family
are eager to do God's will.
May our living the gospel
make us worthy to be called
brothers and sisters of the Lord.
Lord, hear us.

Priest/leader:
With the Lord, there is mercy
and fullness of redemption.
We have prayed with confidence,
aware of all that God has done for us
through Christ our Lord. Amen.

Sunday 10

Sunday 11

Priest/leader:
'I have spoken' says the Lord, 'and I will do it'.
God's word is at work in our world
so we come to the Lord with confidence,
and lay before God our needs
and those of the church and the world.

1. For the gift of humility before God.
(pause)
God takes the initiative.
God makes the weak strong and the strong weak.
We ask for a sense of God's majesty
and the courage to let God rule in our lives.
Lord, hear us.

2. For a desire to please God always.
(pause)
Whether we are alive or dead,
we must be intent on pleasing God.
May we live according to God's law
so that we may be proved worthy
in the law courts of Christ.
Lord, hear us.

3. For an understanding of the mystery of God's kingdom.
(pause)
The kingdom of God is hidden, mysterious and effective.
May we learn to accept God's will in our lives
and by witnessing to gospel values
bring about God's kingdom in our world.
Lord, hear us.

4. For an attitude of thanksgiving to our God.
(pause)
May we always be aware of God's promises in our lives
and be so filled with thanksgiving
that people everywhere may come to acknowledge
the love God has for all the world.
Lord, hear us.

Priest/leader:
Lord, may your kingdom come!
Teach us to be confident in your promises
and grant what we need.
Through Christ our Lord. Amen.

Sunday 11

Sunday 12

Priest/leader:
'Who is this that even the wind and sea obey him?'
With the confidence that comes
from belonging to God's family,
we bring before the Lord
the needs of all the people of the world.

1. For a deeper awareness of the majesty of God.
(pause)
God controls the earth and the sky and the sea.
God is the God of power, the creator of all.
May we grow in understanding God's majesty
and yet be confident
in the presence of the creator God.
Lord, hear us.

2. For an understanding of the love of Christ.
(pause)
The love of Christ overwhelms us.
May we be so filled with an awareness
of what has been achieved for us by Christ
that our lives may bear witness
to his teaching and his example.
Lord, hear us.

3. For a deeper faith in Christ.
(pause)
When we feel afraid and threatened
by forces that are greater than we can bear,
may we be filled with faith in Christ
and be comforted by his power to rescue us.
Lord, hear us.

4. For courage to trust in God's love.
(pause)
In times of great stress and sorrow
- from sickness, loss
and the death of those who love us -
may we turn to our God
and find the consolation that we desire.
Lord, hear us.

Priest/leader:
God of all power and majesty,
be near to us in our times of need.
Remind us of your powerful love
and grant us what we ask.
Through Christ our Lord. Amen.

Sunday 13

Priest/leader:
'Go in peace and be free from your complaint.'
Encouraged by the compassion of Christ
towards those in pain,
we turn to the Lord
in our need.

1. For an appreciation that life is a gift from God.
(pause)
May we thank God always for the gift of life
and may we care for everything that God has made,
avoiding what destroys our world
by what we do and how we live.
Lord, hear us.

2. For a deeper awareness of Christ's generous love.
(pause)
Christ was rich but became poor for our sakes.
May we who live in comfort
be aware of others in need
and imitate the love of Christ
by lives of charity and care.
Lord, hear us.

3. For a love towards those whom society rejects.
(pause)
As Christ was alert to the needs
of the suffering woman,
may we be aware of those who are in need
and, like him, be ready to care
for those who reach out to us.
Lord, hear us.

4. For healing in our lives.
(pause)
May all who are broken or rejected,
alone or in sorrow,
be comforted by the love of Christ
and the care of those in the community
called the church.
Lord, hear us.

Priest/leader:
God of life and love,
fill us with compassion for those in need,
and grant what we ask.
Through Christ our Lord. Amen.

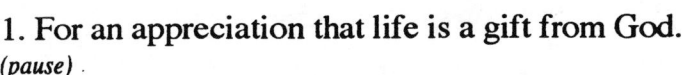

Sunday 14

Priest/leader:
'My grace is enough for you',
says the Lord.
We have been nourished by God's Word
and we turn to the Lord in our need
for ourselves, our church and our world.

1. For the gift to accept prophets among us.
(pause)
May we be accepting of those
whose message is uncomfortable
in our church and in our world,
especially those who remind us of gospel teachings
and the commandments of God.
Lord, hear us.

2. For an awareness of the abundance of God's gifts.
(pause)
In all our needs
- and especially in times of trouble,
sickness and bereavement -
may we be aware of the lavishness of God's grace
and be comforted by the Lord's love.
Lord, hear us.

3. For a renewed eagerness to follow Christ.
(pause)
May we be moved to accept the way of Christ
in our lives
and to be faithful in works of charity towards others
as the Lord commands.
Lord, hear us.

4. For the gift of great faith.
(pause)
May we learn to trust the Lord
and be strong in faith.
May our lives bear witness
to the teaching of the gospel
in what we do and what we value.
Lord, hear us.

Priest/leader:
God of consolation,
strengthen the faith of your people.
Alert us to the prophets in our midst
and show us your will
for the church and the world.
We ask this through Christ our Lord. Amen.

Sunday 14

Sunday 15

Priest/leader:
We are claimed as God's own people,
chosen from the beginning.
Nourished by the Word, broken for us,
we turn to our God in prayer
for ourselves and all God's people.

1. For the gift to accept prophets in our midst.
(pause)
God sends the prophets
to remind us of the commandments
and the way that leads to life.
May we accept the prophets God sends,
calling us to lives of justice and truth and giving.
Lord, hear us.

2. For an awareness of God's generous love.
(pause)
We are a people chosen by God
before the world began.
May we be conscious of God's commandments,
revealed to us in the life and death of Jesus.
Lord, hear us.

3. For a sense of the church's mission.
(pause)
As the apostles were sent to spread the good news,
may we understand that we too share that mission.
May we so live by the teaching of Jesus
that others may come to faith and wholeness.
Lord, hear us.

4. For those who care for the sick.
(pause)
The care of the sick is a mark of God's people
from the earliest days.
We pray for those in our community who are sick and dying
and for those who care for them.
Lord, hear us.

Priest/leader:
God of love,
you command us to resist the desire
for great wealth and possessions.
Teach us to be content with what we have
and to trust in your merciful love.
We ask this through Christ our Lord. Amen.

Sunday 15

Year B

Sunday 16

Priest/leader:
Christ is the peace between us
and through him we have become one people.
Strengthened by God's Word
we come to our living God
with what we need
for our selves, our church and our world.

1. For shepherds and leaders in the church.
(pause)
We pray for those who have authority in the churches
that they may be faithful to the teaching of the gospel
and constantly alert to the promptings
of God's Spirit.
Lord, hear us.

2. For a desire for unity among Christians.
(pause)
In Christ, we have become one people of God.
May we strive for unity among all Christians
that by our common witness and love
people everywhere may come
to the knowledge of the truth.
Lord, hear us.

3. For a desire to find time for God.
(pause)
Just as the apostles were commanded by Christ
to come and rest,
may we find time for God in prayer and in quiet times.
May we relish the times we spend with God
and be strengthened by those times of rest.
Lord, hear us.

4. For those who are searching for the truth.
(pause)
Our world is full of those
who are like sheep without shepherds.
We pray for those who are searching for the truth
about life, about God, about reality.
May they find meaning in the teaching of the gospel
and live in peace and hope and joy.
Lord, hear us.

Priest/leader: God of all peoples,
you are our shepherd
and you care for us always.
Hear the prayers we have made and grant them, we pray,
through Christ our Lord. Amen.

Sunday 16

Sunday 17

Priest/leader:
'There is one Lord, one faith,
one baptism and one God
who is Father of all.'
With confidence in God's love
we bring before the Lord
our needs for the church and for the world.

1. For an attitude of thanksgiving to God.
(pause)
God is the giver of all good things.
May we be conscious of God's goodness to us
in providing food and shelter.
And may we be moved to be generous
to those who need our help.
Lord, hear us.

2. For a right attitude towards others.
(pause)
As God' people, we are commanded
to be charitable, selfless, gentle and patient.
May we learn to practise these virtues
towards others in our community.
Lord, hear us,

3. For a spirit of peace and unity.
(pause)
We are called to unity and peace
by the presence of God's Spirit among us.
May we strive for unity among Christians
by our tolerance and acceptance of others
and learn to live in peace.
Lord, hear us.

4. For a spirit of generosity towards others.
(pause)
Jesus fed the crowds with five loaves and two fish.
May we be generous in sharing what we have
so that people may recognise
the generous love of God
for all the world.
Lord, hear us.

Priest/leader:
God of love,
you created the world and all that it holds.
Teach us to take care of the world
and to share its riches
with one another.
Through Christ our Lord. Amen.

Sunday 17

Year B

Sunday 18

Priest/leader:
'Those who come to me will never be hungry;
those who believe in me will never thirst.'
Nourished and strengthened by God's Word,
we approach the Lord with confidence
presenting our needs and the needs of people everywhere.

1. For a spirit of thanksgiving for God's gifts.
(pause)
May we learn to appreciate God's gifts to us
and to develop an attitude of thanksgiving,
acknowledging the fruitfulness of the earth
and renewing our commitment
to care for God's creation.
Lord, hear us.

2. For a sense of spiritual renewal.
(pause)
We are commanded to put aside our old self
and to be renewed spiritually.
May we be open to God's Spirit
seeking to be faithful to the way of Christ,
living lives of holiness and goodness and truth.
Lord, hear us.

3. For a deepening of faith in Christ.
(pause)
Christ is the way, the truth and the life.
May we grow in faith,
accepting his way as God's way
and his teaching as food for our journey though life.
Lord, hear us.

4. For a desire to share the bread of life.
(pause)
Jesus is the bread that gives life to the world.
By our obedience to Christ
and his commandments,
may we bring others to faith
so that they may share the food
that endures to eternal life.
Lord, hear us.

Priest/leader:
Creator God,
we thank you for the gift of your Son -
Jesus the giver of life.
Increase our faith in him
and grant the prayers we ask.
Through Christ our Lord. Amen.

Sunday 18

Sunday 19

Priest/leader:
'Whoever eats this bread will live for ever.'
We have been fed with the bread that is God's Word
and we now present to the Lord
our prayers for the church and for the world.

1. For an appreciation of God's generosity.
(pause)
God sent an angel to provide food for Elijah.
May we be confident of God's generous love for us
and may we in turn
provide for those who have none.
Lord, hear us.

2. For the gift of forgiveness.
(pause)
We are to forgive one another
as God forgave us in Christ.
May we be tolerant and graceful
in our dealings with one another,
not bearing grudges
but kindness to all.
Lord, hear us.

3. For faith in God's promises.
(pause)
Jesus is the bread of life
and his teaching is the promise of life everlasting.
May we be faithful to his way
and obey his commands
so that we may be raised by the Father
on the last day.
Lord, hear us.

4. For a desire to be of service in the world.
(pause)
We believe that Jesus is the bread of life
given for the life of the world.
May we too be of service to our world,
alert to its needs
and those of all its people.
Lord, hear us.

Priest/leader:
Creator God of all the world,
we confess your Son Jesus
as living bread.
Listen to the prayers we make
through Christ our Lord. Amen.

Year B

Sunday 20

Priest/leader:
'Anyone who eats this bread will live for ever.'
We have listened to God's Word
and been nourished by its teaching.
We now turn to the Lord with confidence
asking what we need
for ourselves, our community and our world.

1. For the gift of wisdom.
(pause)
Wisdom is God's gift of discernment,
teaching us to know what is right
and pleasing to the Lord our God.
May we be persistent in seeking wisdom all our lives
so that we may always walk in the way of the Lord.
Lord, hear us.

2. For simplicity in our lives.
(pause)
May we learn to be content with what we have,
acknowledging the Lord
as the giver of all good things
and constantly giving thanks to God
for the blessings we have in our lives.
Lord, hear us.

3. For a deeper understanding of Jesus, the bread of life.
(pause)
Jesus has promised
that those who eat his flesh and drink his blood
have life for ever.
May our sharing in this Eucharist
be a sign of our deeper commitment
to follow his teaching.
Lord, hear us.

4. For a re-dedication of our lives to Christ.
(pause)
May our belonging to this community
and our celebration of the Mass
be a sign of our faith in Christ
from whom we draw life now and for ever.
Lord, hear us.

Priest/leader:
God of our ancestors,
your son Jesus drew life from you
and we draw life from him.
Consoled by your promises,
we ask you to grant our prayers.
Through Christ our Lord. Amen.

Sunday 20

Sunday 21

Priest/leader:
'You have the message of eternal life.'
We have been strengthened by God's Word
broken for us
and we now turn to the Lord in faith
asking for our needs
and those of the world.

1. For a desire to serve God in the world.
(pause)
Like the leaders of Israel,
we have chosen to serve the Lord our God.
May we be good servants,
active in bringing about God's kingdom
in the world.
Lord, hear us.

2. For those in our community who are married.
(pause)
Married Christians are commanded
to give way to one another in obedience to Christ.
May wives and husbands in our community
grow in love and patience and understanding
in their following of Christ's commands.
Lord, hear us.

3. For perseverance in faith.
(pause)
May we be strong in faith
always choosing to follow the Lord
and confessing him always
as the Holy One of God.
Lord, hear us.

4. For a deeper understanding of the Mass.
(pause)
May we who gather to celebrate the Eucharist
deepen our understanding
of what God has done for us in Christ.
and, being renewed each Sunday ,
live lives of faith and hope and love
according to God's commands.
Lord, hear us.

Priest/leader:
God of all consolation,
you gather your people to teach them your ways
and to remind them of your mighty deeds.
With confidence, we ask you to hear our prayers.
Through Christ our Lord. Amen.

Sunday 22

Priest/leader:
God's Word has been broken for us
and we have been fed by the message
that brings eternal life.
With confidence, we turn to God
and present the needs
of the church and of the world.

1. For a desire to follow God's commandments.
(pause)
May we be faithful in following God's ways
and constant in practising charity and justice
so that others may be drawn to the truth.
Lord, hear us.

2. For justice in our society.
(pause)
May we learn to care for those in need
in the community and in society
following the commands of the Lord
to look after our brothers and sisters
when they come to us in need.
Lord, hear us.

3. For a right understanding of our religion.
(pause)
May we be true followers of Christ,
who taught that religion is not
about human regulations
but about God's command to live lives of justice
and charity towards all.
Lord, hear us.

4. For a desire to keep ourselves true to the gospels.
(pause)
May we always be guided by the gospel
in what we value
and in what we look for in life.
Lord, hear us.

Priest/leader:
God of all goodness,
you command us to be constant
in our following of the gospel.
Make us strong in faith
and grant what we ask
through Christ our Lord. Amen.

Sunday 23

Priest/leader:
'Jesus has done all things well.
He makes the deaf hear and the dumb speak.'
We have been strengthened by God's Word
and professed our faith.
Now we turn to God with confidence
for our needs and those of all peoples.

1. For the gift of courage.
(pause)
Isaiah commands us to have courage
and not to be afraid.
May we be aware of God's power
in our lives and in our world
and have the conviction to live as God wants.
Lord, hear us.

2. For an awareness of God's gifts.
(pause)
God chooses the weak to confuse the strong
and makes them the inheritors of the kingdom.
May we learn to be poor in God's sight
so that we may be rich in faith.
Lord, hear us.

3. For an openness to God's teaching.
(pause)
May our ears be open to hear God's Word
and alert to the prompting of the Spirit
that we may be faithful in living
according to the gospel.
Lord, hear us.

4. For a desire to spread the good news.
(pause)
May we learn to speak clearly
the good news about Jesus Christ
and in our families and communities
speak openly and confidently
about what we believe
and how we are to live.
Lord, hear us.

Priest/leader:
God of all healing,
you make us whole
by the preaching of the gospel.
May we in turn help to bring
that wholeness to all we meet.
We ask this through Christ our Lord. Amen.

Sunday 23

Year B

Sunday 24

Priest/leader:
Those who lose their life for Jesus' sake
and the sake of the gospel will save it.
Nourished by the Word of God,
we bring before the Lord
the needs of the church and the world.

1. For the gift of courage in suffering.
(pause)
Like the servants of God in every age,
may we be of good courage in suffering
and learn to trust in God's goodness
and the care of people in our community.
Lord, hear us.

2. For a desire to please God.
(pause)
Faith without deeds is dead.
May we show forth our faith in God
and be found pleasing to the Lord
by what we do and what we value.
Lord, hear us.

3. For an awareness of how much God loves us.
(pause)
May we continue to grow in our understanding
about how much God loves us
and to recognise the price Jesus paid
to bring us the good news
about God's healing and God's gift of wholeness.
Lord, hear us.

4. For an acceptance of the cross in our lives.
(pause)
May we learn from the example of Jesus
to carry the crosses of life
and so give ourselves for others
as to find that fullness of life we are promised.
Lord, hear us.

Priest/leader:
God of all consolation,
be with those who are suffering.
Give them courage to carry their cross
and us the strength to help them.
We ask this through Christ our Lord. Amen.

Sunday 24

Sunday 25

Priest/leader:
Anyone who welcomes Jesus
welcomes the One who sent him.
We have been fed by God's Word
and now turn to the Lord
for what we need to be a faithful people.

1. For the gift of perseverance.
(pause)
May we be constant in turning from evil,
and holding to what is good.
May we have the grace of perseverance,
resisting those who would lead us into sin
by compromising the gospel
and what is important in life.
Lord, hear us.

2. For those who bring peace in our world.
(pause)
May we be people of peace
in our families and in our communities
and may those who work for peace in our world
be richly blessed by the God of peace.
Lord, hear us.

3. For a desire to be of service in the community.
(pause)
God has called us to be servants rather than masters.
May we learn to follow the example of Jesus
who emptied himself
to become the saving servant of the world.
Lord, hear us.

4. For an appreciation of what is of lasting value.
(pause)
With Jesus as our guide
may we learn what is of lasting value in life
and so live by Jesus' teaching
that people will come to faith
in the God who sent him.
Lord, hear us.

Priest/leader:
Creator God, your son died for us
and rose to bring us wholeness and healing.
May we be imitators of him
in his life of service
in our community and in our world.
We ask this through Christ our Lord. Amen.

Sunday 25

Sunday 26

Priest/leader:
Anyone not against Christ is for Christ.
We have listened to God's Word broken for us
and professed our faith in God.
As God's people we reflect on our needs
and the needs of all the world.

1. For those who are prophets in the world.
(pause)
May we be guided by God's Spirit
to recognise those in our world
who speak the truth
and acknowledge that God's choices
are not limited by our expectations.
Lord, hear us.

2. For a right attitude towards wealth.
(pause)
James teaches us to have a healthy disregard for wealth.
May our richness be measured by our concern for justice
and our wealth reckoned by our concern for the poor.
Lord, hear us.

3. For those who are prophets in the church.
(pause)
May we always be open to prophecy in our time,
welcoming those who remind us of Gospel values
and point us to what God wants
for the community called the church.
Lord, hear us.

4. For an avoidance of scandal in our lives.
(pause)
May we who are older members of the community
try to avoid being obstacles to those who are young.
May we be open to their enthusiasm and imagination
not stifling but encouraging them in the way of the Lord.
Lord, hear us.

Priest/leader:
God of all ages
you are with your people for ever.
Teach us to be faithful followers of your Son
in all we do and say.
We ask this through Christ our Lord. Amen.

Sunday 26

Sunday 27

Priest/leader:
'Anyone who does not receive the kingdom of God
as a little child will never enter it.'
We have listened to God's Word
and professed our faith in God's love.
We open our hearts to the Lord,
recalling our needs.

1. For married people.
(pause)
May we support those who are married in our community
by our prayers and our hospitality.
May we be sensitive and generous towards those
whose marriages are in crisis.
Lord, hear us.

2. For those who are suffering or in need.
(pause)
Through his suffering, Jesus has entered his glory.
May we who are his brothers and sisters
persevere in hope
comforting those who are suffering
by our patience, our care and our love.
Lord, hear us.

3. For a child-like attitude towards God's kingdom.
(pause)
May we be like children in welcoming the kingdom
- full of hope and joy and anticipation -
eager to do what God wants
and acknowledging our dependence on the Lord.
Lord, hear us,

4. For those who are divorced.
(pause)
May we be compassionate to those
whose marriages have failed
and welcome them with love in our communities.
May we learn to support them
as they seek to rebuild their lives.
Lord, hear us

Priest/leader:
God of love
you teach us that we must be like children
in welcoming your reign in our lives.
Help us to be open to your guiding Spirit
and to renew each day our hope in you.
We ask this through Christ our Lord. Amen

Sunday 27

Year B

Sunday 28

Priest/leader:
'For God, all things are possible.'
We are encouraged and strenghened
by the Word of God
and as followers of Jesus
we bring our needs to the Father.

1. For the gift of wisdom.
(pause)
May we be given the gift of wisdom
to help us have good priorities in our lives
that reflect the teaching of Jesus
and the values of the kingdom of God.
Lord, hear us.

2. For a love of God's Word.
(pause)
God's Word is alive and active.
May we learn to love God's Word
and to proclaim its teaching
in how we live and what we value.
Lord, hear us.

3. For a right attitude towards riches.
(pause)
May we be guided by Gospel teaching
in our attitude towards wealth
tempering our need for money and security
with a desire to be generous as God commands.
Lord, hear us.

4. For generosity in working for the kingdom.
(pause)
May we be generous with our time and resources
in working to establish God's rule in our world
and to be constant in our witness
to God's truth and justice and love.
Lord, hear us.

Priest/leader:
God of love
you are the giver of all good things.
Fill us with confidence in you
that we may be faithful witnesses of your kingdom.
We ask this through Christ our Lord. Amen.

Sunday 28

Sunday 29

Priest/leader:
The letter to the Hebrews encourages us to be confident
in approaching the throne of grace.
We turn to God, then,
asking that we need
for ourselves, our families, our church and our world.

1. For a right understanding of suffering.
(pause)
The servant of God in Isaiah
took on the faults of many
and suffered for them.
May we continue to struggle with suffering in our world
and be generous, compassionate and supportive
towards those who are in need.
Lord, hear us.

2. For renewed confidence in God.
(pause)
Christ is our High Priest, the Son of God.
With him as our guide and our brother
may we be renewed in confidence
especially in times of trouble and suffering.
Lord, hear us.

3. For perseverance in witnessing to what we believe.
(pause)
May we persevere in living according to the commandments
and the teaching of Jesus
especially when it is unfashionable
to proclaim Gospel values
and even more difficult to live by them.
Lord, hear us.

4. For a desire to be of service.
(pause)
May we follow the example of Jesus
who came not to be served but to serve.
May we be alert to the needs of others in our community
and generous in our service towards them.
Lord, hear us.

Priest/leader:
God of all consolation,
teach us to be good servants in your kingdom
and to imitate your son
in a spirit of acceptance, tolerance and giving.
We ask this through Christ our Lord. Amen.

Sunday 29

Year B

Sunday 30

Priest/leader:
'Courage! The Lord is calling you.'
Strengthened by God's Word broken for us
we come in confidence to the Lord
with our needs and those of our world.

1. For the gift of being comforters.
(pause)
Just as God comforted the people of Israel
so may we be comforters of one another
rich in hospitality and care
warm in our welcoming
and strong in our support of each other.
Lord, hear us.

2. For confidence in God's goodness and love.
(pause)
Christ is our High Priest
who pleads for us with the Father.
May his presence with God
renew our confidence in prayer
and our desire to love.
Lord, hear us.

3. For those who are seeking the truth.
(pause)
May those who are looking for truth
experience the healing touch of the Lord
and, being filled with courage,
acknowledge Jesus as Saviour and Lord.
Lord, hear us.

4. For persistence in following the Lord.
(pause)
May we be couragous in following the Lord
obedient to the teaching of the Gospel
and persistent in lives that show forth
the love and care that Jesus showed
to the blind man.
Lord, hear us.

Priest/leader:
God of light
help us to see more clearly
the way you have planned for us.
Give us courage and perseverance
as we follow you in our lives.
We ask this through Christ our Lord. Amen.

Sunday 30

Sunday 31

Priest/leader:
'You are not far from the kingdom of God.'
God's Word has been broken for us
and we have professed our faith.
Now with confidence we turn to God
for all our needs.

1. For God's love to be shown forth in our lives.
(pause)
We are commanded to love God
all the days of our lives.
May we be constant in keeping God's commandments
and may the desire to serve God
be written in our hearts.
Lord, hear us.

2. For a devotion to Christ the High Priest.
(pause)
Christ is our High Priest who remains with God for ever.
May we always acknowledge
Christ's powerful presence with God
and pray always in his name.
Lord, hear us.

3. For a desire to love our neighbour as ourselves.
(pause)
Jesus teaches us that we love God by loving one another.
May we grow in love of one another,
learning to forgive, to accept, to tolerate
and to grow together into the people that God wants.
Lord, hear us.

4. For a longing for the kingdom of God.
(pause)
May we be filled with a great desire
for God's kingdom to come.
May our struggle for justice and peace
and our concern for truth
be signs of our intense longing for God's will to be done.
Lord, hear us.

Priest/leader:
God of love
fill us with your blessings
so that we will be strong
in keeping your commandments
and constant in loving one another.
We ask this through Christ our Lord. Amen.

Sunday 31

Year B

Sunday 32

Priest/leader:
'Christ is the presence of God on our behalf.'
God's Word is broken for us
and we have made our act of faith.
Now, with Christ, we turn to God
recalling our needs.

1. For the gift of hospitality.
(pause)
Like the woman who welcomed Elijah
may we be a people of hospitality,
welcoming strangers into our community
with warmth and acceptance.
Lord, hear us.

2. For trust in God's merciful love
(pause)
The letter to the Hebrews teaches that all will be judged.
Trusting in God's merciful love
may we be comforted that Christ
took on our faults
and promises salvation to those who wait for him.
Lord, hear us.

3. For the gift of sincerity.
(pause)
Jesus condemned the hypocrisy of his enemies.
May we too avoid hypocrisy
in our dealings with one another
and treat all people
with sincerity and honesty.
Lord, hear us.

4. For a spirit of trust in the Lord.
(pause)
May we learn to trust in God's goodness,
and providential care of us
so that we may find peace with what we have
and be generous towards others.
Lord, hear us.

Priest/leader:
God of love
you sent your son to be our saviour and our teacher.
Open our hearts to his voice
and our minds to follow his example.
We ask this through Christ our Lord. Amen.

Sunday 32

Sunday 33

Priest/leader:
'Heaven and earth will pass away
but my words will stand.'
We have listened to the Bible readings,
God's Word broken for our nourishment.
Now we turn with confidence
for our needs and those of the church and the world.

1. For openness to the signs of the times.
(pause)
May we acknowledge that God is the ruler of the universe
and only God knows what will happen to the world.
May we be filled with confidence and trust
as we await the coming of the Lord.
Lord, hear us.

2. For an understanding of what Christ has achieved for us.
(pause)
May we grow in understanding the work of Christ,
who offered himself to destroy sin for ever;
and by lives that are faithful to his teaching
may we seek the perfection that God desires.
Lord, hear us.

3. For confidence in times of trial.
(pause)
May we never despair in times of suffering
in the church and in the world,
recognising that God is Lord of the universe
and that all things are in God's hands.
Lord, hear us.

4. For joy in doing God's will.
(pause)
Even in times of confusion and unrest
may we find joy and peace
in knowing that we are doing God's will
by our obedience to the commandments
and the way of Christ.
Lord, hear us.

Priest/leader
Eternal God,
our first beginning and our last end,
fill us with hope and confidence
and trust in your goodness.
We ask this through Christ our Lord. Amen.

Sunday 33

Sunday 34   Feast of Christ the King

Priest/leader
'Jesus came to bear witness to the truth.'
In this festival of Christ the King,
we have listened to God's Word
and now turn to God with confidence
for all our needs.

1. For an understanding of the authority of Christ.
(pause)
May we deepen our understanding of Christ our King
acknowledging his authority in all the earth;
may our lives reflect gospel teaching
and attract all people to his gentle rule.
Lord, hear us.

2. For an understanding of the majesty of Christ.
(pause)
Christ is the first born of the dead,
the ruler of those who rule the earth.
May we grow in understanding his majesty
and rejoice that we can serve him
in the church and in the community.
Lord, hear us.

3. For an acceptance of Christ our King.
(pause)
Christ's kingdom is not of this world.
May we be true servants of Christ our King
in promoting gospel values
and working for the rule of God.
Lord, hear us.

4. For a desire to bear witness in the world.
(pause)
May we follow the example of Christ the King
bearing witness to the truth of the gospel
by what we profess and how we live.
Lord, hear us.

Priest/leader:
Lord of the universe,
your son Jesus established a kingdom
of justice, love and peace.
Help us to live according to his teaching
for he is Lord, for ever and ever. Amen.

Sunday 34

Feast of Saint Peter and Saint Paul

Priest/leader:
'I will give you the keys of the kingdom of heaven!'
We have been comforted by God's Word
on this festival of Saints Peter and Paul.
We turn to God with confidence
in prayer for the church and the world.

1. For the people of God everywhere.
(pause)
May we be faithful in following the way of Christ
and be guided by the teaching of the apostles
who were the first preachers
of the good news about Jesus.
Lord, hear us.

2. For Christian leaders.
(pause)
May Christian leaders be strong in faith
and hope and love,
alert to the signs of the times
as they proclaim the gospel in today's world.
Lord, hear us.

3. For Christian teachers and thinkers.
(pause)
May Christian teachers be constant in searching for the truth
of what God wants for the church and the world.
May they be inspired by the example of Paul
who persevered to the end in faith.
Lord, hear us.

4. For tolerance and unity among Christians.
(pause)
May we learn from the example of Peter and Paul
to be generous in love towards one another
and seek that unity and tolerance
to which they witnessed.
Lord, hear us.

Priest/leader:
God of all ages
we praise you for the witness of Peter and Paul.
Grant the prayers we make this day.
Through Christ our Lord. Amen

Assumption of the Blessed Virgin Mary

Priest/leader:
'The last enemy to be destoyed is death.'
Today we celebrate Christ's victory over sin and death,
and the assumption of the Blessed Virgin Mary
is a great sign of that victory.
Confident that we too share that promise
we turn to the Lord in prayer.

1. For hope in God's promises.
(pause)
May we be filled with confidence in God's power
and be assured that we too will share
the glory that has been promised.
Lord, hear us.

2. For thanksgiving for the life of Mary the Virgin.
(pause)
Mary is the woman adorned by the sun,
standing on the moon,
a crown of stars on her head.
May we be thankful to God
that she is also the faithful one
who wanted always to do God's will.
Lord, hear us.

3. For a desire to imitate Mary the Virgin.
(pause)
Mary proclaimed the greatness of the Lord.
May she be for us a constant example of the way of Christ
by her openness to God and her care for others.
Lord, hear us.

4. For a renewed faith in God's plan for our lives.
(pause)
God chose Mary to be the Mother of the Saviour.
We too have a place in God's plan of salvation.
May we be faithful followers of Christ
so that, by Mary's prayers,
we too may share the glory of the Resurrection.
Lord, hear us.

Priest/leader:
God of all creation,
you raised Mary to glory
and she is our queen and mother.
Listen to our prayers on this feast of the Assumption
and grant what we ask.
Through Christ our Lord. Amen

Assumption

Feast of All Saints

Priest/leader:
On this feast of All Saints
we gather to praise God.
The Word has been broken for us
and we ask God for what we need.

1. For a spirit of joy.
(pause)
May we be filled with joy this day
as we celebrate the glory of the saints
praising God for their lives and example
and pledging ourselves to follow their way.
Lord, hear us.

2. For contentment in God's service.
(pause)
May we be content to live as God's people
at peace in doing God's will
knowing that the kingdom is promised
to those who are faithful to the end.
Lord, hear us.

3. For a desire to live as God wants.
(pause)
May we be the people of the beatitudes
taking its teaching to our hearts
and living out the values it contains
by lives of integrity, honesty and love.
Lord, hear us.

4. For all God's people.
(pause)
May we be accepting of all God's people
who want to belong to the kingdom
and may we work for that unity and peace
that are the promised marks of the followers of Christ.
Lord, hear us.

Priest/leader:
God of all saints
we bless you and thank you
for their lives and witness.
Bless our efforts to live as your people.
We ask this through Christ our Lord. Amen.

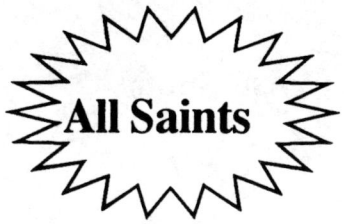

Year B

All Souls

Priest/leader:
'I will raise then up on the last day.'
We worship God on this feast of all souls
and bring before the Lord our concerns
our needs and our memories.

1. For a firm faith in the promises of God.
(pause)
May we renew our faith in God
who has been faithful to the promises
made in the past
and with a firm trust in God's goodness
commend ourselves to the care of the Lord.
Lord, hear us.

2. For hope in the resurrection.
(pause)
Jesus has promised to raise us up on the last day.
Today may we be filled with hope in the resurrection
promised to us and to all those who believe in him.
Lord, hear us.

3. For those who have died.
(pause)
We pray for those who have died
in the blessed hope of resurrection
that they may see God in whom they believed
and enjoy God's presence forever.
Lord, hear us.

4. For those who mourn.
(pause)
May those who are in mourning
grieving those who have died
be comforted by their faith and hope
and by the loving care of others in the community.
Lord, hear us.

Priest/leader:
God of all ages,
to you a thousand years is like a day.
Be close to us as we recall our dead.
Comfort us with your gifts of faith and hope.
We ask this through Christ our Lord. Amen.

All Souls